This Side of Time

This Side of Time

Poems by Ko Un

Translated by
Clare You and Richard Silberg

Introduction by Lewis Lancaster

Korean Voices Series, Volume 16

WHITE PINE PRESS / BUFFALO, NEW YORK

Publication of this book was made possible, in part, with public funds from the New York State Council on the Arts, a State Agency, and from the National Endowment for the Arts, which believes that a great nation deserves great art; and by a generous grant from the Sunshik Min Endowment for the Advancement of Korean Literature at the Korea Institute, Harvard University.

First Edition.

ISBN: 978-1-935210-32-0

Printed and bound in the United States of America.

Library of Congress Control Number: 2011931996

White Pine Press
P.O. Box 236, Buffalo, New York 14201
www.whitepine.org

CONTENTS

Introduction

Ko Un came to the University of California, Berkeley in 1997 for a reading of his poetry. At that time Professor Robert Hass, then Poet Laureate of the United States, gave a moving tribute to Ko Un. In his address, he called to mind his first sight of the poet in 1986, participating in a rally with college students. As I listened to Prof. Hass, I thought that Ko Un is one of those rare individuals who is met and never forgotten. Allen Ginsberg started his Foreword to *Beyond Self* with the mention of his first meeting and Thich Nhat Hanh follows suit in his Foreword with a reference to the initial contact. I am the same; my memory of the first meeting is still vivid. There is something about him that makes the first meeting so memorable; we always refer to it.

In 1987, Berkeley was the site of a large international conference on Buddhist Christian Dialogue. As one of the organizing group, I was approached by a graduate student, who asked that we consider inviting a Buddhist poet to the meeting. It seemed to be a good idea to provide a variety of voices for the Buddhist side of the dialogue, and so we decided to include Ko Un in the conference. It was not a simple matter. For two decades, he had been a prominent protestor against the military governments of Korea. In 1980, his outspoken opposition was used to send him to prison and to torture. He was released from his sentence in 1982, and while he was less strident, the government viewed him with suspicion. When he asked for a passport and permission to travel to Berkeley for the conference, his request was denied. For some weeks, we attempted to help him with the visa and travel documents. Letters flowed to the California members of Congress and to the Korean Embassy. Telephone calls to and from Korea were happening in the middle of the night. We decided to persevere in this project and to do our utmost to overcome the obstacles to his travel. Finally, two days before the event, he was given a passport and managed to get to Berkeley… after the opening of the conference but in time for his panel. We were surprised to find him a quiet and kindly person, who read poems that touched on themes of insight and compassion. His voice, sometimes a mere whisper as he recited his verse, held the audience enthralled. While his words were often delivered in a low voice, the intensity of his feelings roared out to all of us. He painted a picture for us of delusion and suffering in the midst of the emptiness of thoughts and experience. Here was a man who had suffered for his poetry, and yet it still came from him with every breath. I don't remember the other papers of that conference fifteen years ago, but I can return again and again to that room, quieted by his poetry and force of spirit. We find that he revisits those prison experiences and in this volume writes

> If you're tortured
> you know a human is inhuman.
> Both the torturer
> and the tortured
> deep at night in the second basement room.

When he came to Berkeley, it was his first trip abroad. Since then he has been a world traveler going to the continents of the world with their large cities and remote deserts and mountains. One of his poems expresses his response to these distant and exotic places.

> So long as there's a hometown
> you're not free,
> not in the Siberia of your heart,
> not in the Gobi Desert.

His insights call us back to ourselves and the limitations that exist because we have attachments.

Over the past decade, it has been my pleasure to meet with Ko Un in Berkeley and in Korea. The times we have spent drinking coffee or eating meals together are made special by his poetic urge. Many times, when we have talked about our personal lives, he will suddenly glow with delight and take out a pad of paper and write down a line or an idea for a future poem. At first, this amused me and also puzzled me because I could see little significance in the comments that I had made. Over time, his delight in an idea or an image has shown me that our lives are filled with unrecognized moments of beauty and meaning

Like many poets, he delights in nature and the observation of it. The imagery goes beyond the words to a visual delight as in his remembrance of an event:

> As the crane takes off
> the pine branches where it sat rebound.
> It's said,
> the pine started after it but stopped.

His insights are not limited to the beauty of mountains, streams, and birds. He writes his poetry from the everyday experience of thousands of urban dwellers who live in high rise apartment towers. Looking out of their windows they can see hundreds of other windows where unknown and unmet people are dwelling. As Ko Un experiences this, his poem gives vent to a moment of compassion for those anonymous and often unseen people:

> 1:30 AM
>
> The light went out in Unit 506 on the 18th floor.
> Across
> on the 19th floor, the light in 706 went out soon after.

Sleep well.
Get to know each other tomorrow.

It takes the insightful vision of the poet to pounce on these moments and hold them up for view. When I shared with him the story of my mother's death and her last days of voluntary fasting, he smiled and said, "Yes, that's it, that's it!" It was left to me to discover the meaning of what he saw and what he said. Little wonder that I treasure these times with him and learn much about myself and life. One line from his poem "Son Room" stays with me:

Simply play for a while with troubles, illusions, then stand up

I think that enlightenment would be mine, if I could smile and say, "Yes, that's it, that's it."

What is this mountain clothed in fall leaves!
A Fire.
A fire
of innocence.

— Lewis Lancaster

LITTLE SONGS
from *Poems Left Behind*

It's cold!
That sharpens my wits.

Standing barefoot on spring earth,
a flower buds from the crown of my head.

At the edge of a reed field,
a mallard, preparing to leave,
preens its neck feathers all day.

Grim frosty morning,
nowhere to put my feet, I stumped back in.

You, leaves still green on the hill,
wither away!

My fifty year old wife is my friend.
My sixty year old husband is my friend.
The children are all gone.
Just these two.

At dusk they walked the road to the sea
over the hill leisurely.
They were long and beautiful in the sunset.

I signaled as I sailed
through the strait of Ch'uja-do, the vacant island.

The rocks covered with seagull droppings
were my answer.
The comet vanished.
It glinted, then sparked out
as the sun stood
above the Earth.

Zen Master Imje roars.
Master Duksan plies his big stick
and the mountain in front flips
to become the mountain behind.

Master shout!
Master hit!

Zen Master Imje (Linji in Chinese, Rizai in Japanese) lived in China c. 800–867 and developed a reputation as the "master of the shout." The lineage of his school was one of the main inflluences of Zen in Japan, named the Rinzai Sect.

Duksan (780–865 CE) (Deshan or Te-shan in Chinese; Toku-san in Japanese) is one of the greatest Zen Master in history. There are many stories about him striking his disciples with a stick in his younger days.

I asked the tide:

Tell me,
after leaving Jungsun, A-uraji,
when did you arrive?
When will you leave
and make ripples
before Yunpyung Island in the western sea?

I should follow you down,
I know, you charted the best way.
That day, departing the world, waving your hands.

Old man in a charcoal-hut
in the Hwenggye Mountains of Kangwon Province, you must be
lonely.
Loneliness is my pal.

Winds blow woo-hoo-hoo.
I see a threadbare short skirt hanging on the line,
where's your daughter?

She must've gone to find mushrooms in these back hills or
somewhere
a few years ago.

As the crane takes off
the pine branches where it sat rebound.
It's said,
the pine started after it but stopped.

If she doesn't understand what I say
I'm a foreigner.
If I don't get her silence
she is just a mute.

A thousand miles between us.
Next to me
they exchange talks about the deceased.
Some wine is left,
but the appetizers are gone.
Could death be an appetizer for the living?

I heard "Boom!"
like the sound of a boulder crashing.

Could that be the voice of the dusky mountain?
The owl's eyes
got wider.

The worm I used to play with
spoke,
"No matter who calls you,
don't be so quick to say 'yes.'
Most likely it's not for you."

The ear that's deaf to a sick child's whimper,
what could it hear?

The fall dragonfly wings vibrate without a sound.

Is there an afterlife for being remorseful?
My poor old mule,
next time I'll be the mule
and carry you on my back
down a long road.

In the barn, the sick horse stands to the end,
the dawn is breaking in the distance.
It was a long night,
a long night.

Grandpa punctuated his talk.
"It's a long way to travel.
Don't be in a rush,
stride like an ox.
Take a rest now and then."

The autumn leaves fall dancing.
I'll dance my way out too
when it's time to leave this world.

Do I have a love
to wash away people's hate?
I opened an umbrella
then closed it, and
let the rain fall down on me.

I asked a child,
"Do you want to be a beggar
or a thief?"

The child asked back,
"Is that all there is
in the world?"

"Yeah, that's all. Only the Caspian and the Black Sea."

It's not just Pakyon Cascade tumbling down,
the sunlight crashes scattering
over the Pankyon Cascade.

I'm still a bum.

What bird songs have you got
in your heart?
My ear's pulled down to your breast.

At the Delphi shrine

I became an oracle.
Eighty-two year old poet
Lawrence Fellinghetti became one, too.

A knife danced and the drum beat for a long time.

Spring snow falls on me.
Catching a cold
like love,
I let the spring snow fall on this skinny body.

Yelling for thirty years,
let them go now.

Justice
among them,
set it free!

Maybe because of the long voyage of the Yellow Sea Kingfish
my body is worn out.
I fell deep asleep
near Sunyu Island of Kogunsan.

Mother kangaroo
and her baby
were waiting in unison for someone
in a suburb of Darwin in Northern Australia.

At Auschwitz in Poland
the mounds of eyeglass frames,
the mounds of shoes there,
mounds of de-soul-ation.

I looked down on the Mongol desert in March,
it was like father
it was like mother's face.

More than anything I felt shame.

On the trash by the road
a thrown-out fan
was turning in cold wind.
It fanned fiercely.

I stopped for a long time.

A wild boar is playing with a shark,
a tortoise with a nightingale
in the deep ravine.

I, too, will play with Comrade Park Jisup
in Kimchaek City of the North.

Kimchaek City: The city named after Kim Il Sung's friend Kim Chaek

Is only the time that compounds interest cruel?
Is time for lust less cruel?
Compassionate time,
I beg you not to sojourn in this land.

Ten, thirty or sixty years,
if our time were not so fleeting,
if our lives were not so short-lived,
humans would've stayed an extra primitive horde.

Ah, long live the noble transitory!

Today
though it's an ordinary day
a man is born
a man dies
a man is waiting.

Today, the setting sun glows boldly into sundown.

Forget it!
To let you forget, the crescent moon slips behind a cloud.

Rhododendron is in bloom.
Over there the crepe-myrtle sulks bloomlessly.
In this way, the world holds each life in its own life;
I wander in glee.

Yi Munjae, reporting on the Diamond Mountains marathon,
        said:

He saw
the snow
like snow flowing out of the steamer,
falling
neatly,
suffering martyrdom,
layer on layer
piling up.

He also
learned
snow's whiteness,
true whiteness
as snow baring snow each to each.

It was good!

Those that lived through cruel cold
as if it were nothing,
after today's rain, they are thoroughly soaked.
The trees,
dirt,
roots in the earth, and
the dazzling sounds of water.

Near Inwol of Namwon
on this side of time
a wayside grave spoke,

Hey,
are you passing by without noticing me?

I'm Yu Hong-yeol,
the Yu Hong-yeol of Yi Hyun-sang squad who shot at you face
to face
in the Bitjom Valley battle.

Namwon is a historic city of romance and Inwol market place in the south-west of Korea.

Yi Hyung-sang was the communist revolutionary or guerilla leader in South Korea during the Korea War. Who shot him dead in the Bitjom Valley, South Korea in 1953, remains unsolved.

For no reason
one giggled,
the other almost sobbed.
They
are buried, leaving their laughs and cries behind.

The graves covered with snow.

No anguish left in me. The candle's out.

For an elephant,
for a chimpanzee, there's sorrow.
I have no sorrow.

The '60's old anguish,
the '70's,
the '80's new hope.

None of these now; I stand before a pig-head at the South Gate
Market.

I took a nap yesterday.
I took a nap today.
I'm going crazy.

At night I can't stop thinking about Hölderlin.

The world is the crucible of power.
Look at the fascism of the labor union.
Look at the demands of the villagers.
Look at the editorials of the major papers.

Forty years old.
Fifty years old.
These men have no place to go.
Monday, Wednesday they leave the house,
for nothing.

Koan is a trap, a ditch.
A tiger got stuck in the ditch and can't get out.

   Idiot Koan!

A FEW SMALL SONGS
from Late Songs

Little flowers
delicately pinned here and there
in the grass.

Proud quilt as if just sewn by machine.

Even the sunlight knows it.

If wisdom's
not love,
love is
not wisdom,
wash them
off our hands.

A breeze startled the calf from its doze.

Look at the old man!

Once,
when Iran's Tehran oil pipeline was laid,
didn't he wallow in lust all night?
Once during the Libyan desert pipeline construction
 in the sweltering 104 degree heat,
didn't he curse them as the pipes were carried in?

The sun's going down; the darkness deepening.

1:30 AM

The light went out in Unit 506 on the 18th floor.
Across
on the 19th floor, the light in 706 went out soon after.

Sleep well.
Get to know each other tomorrow.

Go into the hothouse, Oga,
that's like a mother,
like an aunt,
and talk to yourself.
There's still a lot to talk about in this world.

Oga is a girl's name

The neighbor's sick baby's crying.
We
should not hate one another.

I love August.
I love the August sun.
I remember ten billion years ago.

Ah, my body is smeared with primeval light.

MORE SMALL SONGS
from Full of Shame

PLASTIC BAG

A black plastic bag
that held two bundles of scallions,

emptied

it rose and danced solo
in a wisp of wind.
It danced and
flew over the fence sloppily.

Mother!

EAR

Over this world
someone's coming from another world.

The sound of night rain.

Someone's leaving for that other world. The two are sure to
meet.

TO HARYONG

Strange – winds're down. The weeds have stopped weeping.

Brook sounds
whisper to one another.

The boat on the sea
still doesn't know where.

Unwritten poems are poemier.

Haryong is Ko Un's wife.

HERE AND THERE

A name for this,
a name for that.
Again
a name for that one.
I'm thirsty.

One man's lie
spread across ten thousand people
and became a thrashed-out truth,

shit on the wind.

Here

the names piled
between eyes glare
with puffing hates
with love,

useless.

There,

a lonesome flower.

FALL LEAVES I

My spring, my summer days,
half my life,
I can never be you
in the wretched half remaining.

Look!
Look

at the falling oak leaves – four, five, six . . .

FALL LEAVES II

What is this mountain clothed in fall leaves!
A fire.
A fire

of innocence.

EMPTY BODY

In the years served
the convicts
ran out naked in the morning.
As they ran
what they hid in their asses
fell out.

They ran, laughing
ha,
ha,
ha,
with open mouths.
What they hid in their mouths
fell out.

Cell to the factory,
the factory to the cell,
the naked body
came
and went like that.

Better to spend the days watching the lifer,
that will do you.
Soon a seven-year term,
a four-year term will be up.

Ha,
ha,

ha,
that's how he enters the world,
empty body.

Empty body that's how
he leaves the world.

LOOKING BACK

The fall has come and gone a thousand times.
Baby,
baby,
I
had a new-born smile, too.

THIEVES

Guests always arrive on the peninsula
from the continent,
from the sea.

If they were really guests, how happy we'd be—
we'd rush out barefoot to welcome them.

Flat-out thieves!

ON THE PEAK OF MANJANG

What I said
was already spoken by another.

What I shouted,
waving my arm,
was already spoken by another.

I look down from the mountain top.

Where
are my words?

Even my cries were someone else's. Absolutely no I.

Manjang is one of the Bukhan Mountain peaks near Seoul

PRIDE

For me there's no temple, no shrine today.

I believe nothing.
Desperately, tonight
I fight off the neon lie.

My ancestral arrowheads still tremble.

WHITE BUTTERFLY

Here look
at the ocean's foolish face,
wisdom's ghost,
a white butterfly flutters over.

The world's books are all closed.

HER FATHER

The day Daughter arrived,
the geranium pots of six
all flowered.

The day Daughter left,
I cut my old finger carelessly.

BABY FLOUNDER

Despair of a baby flounder,
just hooked.
Rising to the surface
it flaps its tail with all its might,
pulls the line taut in the setting sun.
The hope in despair.

A SELF PORTRAIT

At the border
between word and word.
there's a helpless man who can't come or go.

The poet, words' bastard child.

THIS WORLD

The pond
will soon bloom with lotus flowers.
In its depths
horrific life and death abound.

This world is not just mother, not just father.

YEARNING

Awakened,
I hear the thunder rumble away.

It will be forty years
since Father died.
Ten years soon
for Mother.

After the thunder it rains. Then the leaves wake up, swish, swish.

TO YOU

Don't worry!
It's the wind rising again. Empty branches dance.

TO YOU AGAIN

Underwater
the gang of fish.

Above
the seagulls.

Just like my hometown, ho—ho—

BEAR

Look,
the old bear coming back to the world
after her winter rest.

A baby
on her back
crawling.

Some day I want to crawl like that,
slow,
so slow.

YEARNING FOR HOME

What joy for baby to stand on two legs.
What joy for Mother.
But
 two legs is the beginning of corruption.
Mountain is mountain.
Sea is sea.
Ah- when can I go back on all fours?

OKINAWA

Where a baby's born calmly
during Typhoon Ida.
Where it cries lustily
after it's born.
I want to be born again
from their women's waters.
Oh my many mistakes!

The hungry child was crying,
and the sick child,
and the child who lost its mother.

I was crying, too, at seventy-three.

MOONY NIGHT

Until now
I've lived
with you.
No,
until now
I've lived off
you.

Moon!

Mother passed away.
As for my sister,
I don't know if she's dead or alive.

Moon! I'm a shameless hooligan. Just shine off!

ON DOKDO ISLAND

I came to shout your name.
Shouting to you,
I fan out your thousand years
to the world.
.

Dokdo Island of the Eastern Sea.

THE SOUND OF NIGHT RAIN

A thousand years ago you're me,
and a thousand years from now you're me.
Together you and I are listening
to the sound of night rain.

FIVE SIJO

My first five Sijos

1. WILD PIGEONS

It wasn't the Muyoung Pagoda
   nor the Dabo Pagoda.
It was a threadbare dwarf pagoda at the edge
   of a field of weeds.
All that came and went over the mountain pass were wild
   pigeons.

2. NOW
July 2007

The roof was washed away,
   the beam got buried.
You can't see the hill behind,
   and the village in front is gone.
All alone an eighty-year-old grandma
   can't find her dead grandson.

3. A POPLAR TREE

I stood all day
      tight-lipped in hard winds.
I came through the storm
     with eyes closed.
At last the windstorm died down,
      ten thousand leaves sprang up.

4. ON THE BAEKNOK LAKE

The rock, hard-won stand
     at Halla crater lake,
as four seas surge up behind
     a screen of cloud,
the ten thousand waves in my dream
     flow on and on.

5. ON THE SACRED BAEKDU MOUNTAIN PEAK

As I climb with a full heart
   up to Baekdu Peak at dawn,
the sun rising in the east,
   moon setting in the west,
is the sky opening up,
   shining on this people?

CRESCENT MOON

Too well off, no time to watch the crescent moon.
Oh my humble sadness toward the universe!

BABY'S CRY

Fella, let me spank your butt.
In your cry, "wau-ah"
the world is new again.

STARS

The stars and I are plotting a revolution
                because the universe is being mismanaged.

FORGET-ME-NOT

This land's long long summer,
wherever you go
an abundance of forget-me-nots
like exploitation
slavering away.

FATHER

Food in his kids' mouth, that's Nirvana!

FIVE DAY MARKET

Hubbub of the market place,
you're the Sutra; you're the Bible.

PARTING

Parting from its mom
the baby bird is free at last.
Get away.
Get away.
Get away.

ONE WHO HAS TO LEAVE

He's going.
He's going.
He who has to
sadly,
so far so good —

SHAMAN

Traitors of this era become
gods of the next.
The shaman who worships all first spirits is right.
Right on, sway on.

GRASS

My father lives here
on this hill covered with my country's grass.
His friends live here.
Twenty years since their deaths.

LATE AUTUMN

Crows and magpies are together
in the vacant field.
Being together, the free with the free.

HOMETOWN

So long as there's a hometown
you're not free,
not in the Siberia of your heart,
not in the Gobi Desert.

CANNA

Red canna of mid-summer
I want you to punish me,
my escapism,
my vanity,
the hypocrisy of my name

COLD WATER

A drink of cold water in the morning,
let this poverty stay, I pray
facing the East.

NAEJANG MOUNTAIN

Sick brother, let go and die
after you see next year's fall leaves.

STONES

If you're in love,
even stones become lovers.
Throw a stone
and fill the world.

THE GLOW OF THE SETTING SUN

I've forgotten you
glow of my fatherland,
glow of the setting sun
when all whores turn back to virgins.

KIDDY TIME

Chased by the shower
I fell to the ground.

As the sun went down
I counted the stars.
When I got hungry
my three tape worms acted up.

MORNING BIRDSONG

I didn't die –waking up I hear that.

REGULAR GUY

We trust there is sun
when it's covered by clouds.
We believe in the world
even though we all die.
We believe in this world of trees and grass.

BREEZE

Only you can make a mountain a field

Breeze!
Invincible!

TORTURE

If you're tortured
you know a human is inhuman.
Both the torturer
and the tortured
deep at night in the second basement room.

A DAY

Open your eyes! Each sentient being
reveals its colors at night,
the far distant mountain, the near mountain,
even my wife's calling voice.

LOVER

When you long for your lover,
each being is precious.
Each precious — even pigs and the dog's fleas.

THE CRAZY

There must be a fella who says
the sun rises in the west.
He wakes up the world.
You, crazy one,
come to this land of facade.

Ko Un

Ko Un is one of the best-known poets in Korea and abroad, and has been nominated several times for the Nobel Prize in Literature. He is a prolific author with over one hundred volumes of poetry as well as many volumes of fiction and non-fiction in his native Korean. His work has been widely translated into many languages, including a number of works in English translation such as *The Three Way Tavern, Beyond Self, Ten Thousand Lives, Songs for Tomorrow,* and *Little Pilgrim.* Ko Un was imprisoned several times during the military government in Korea and lived for a decade as a Zen Monk before returning to the secular world. He teaches Korean poetry amd literature at Seoul National University.

Richard Silberg

Richard Silberg was born in New York City in 1942. He received his B.A. from Harvard in 1963 and his M.A. in Creative Writing from San Francisco State University in 1973. He is Associate Editor of *Poetry Flash* and Co-Director of the Poetry Flash poetyry reading series in Berkeley. He also taught "Writing and Appreciating Contemporary Poetry" and poetry workshops at University of California Berkeley Extension. His first book was a volume of speculative social philosophy, *The Devolution of the People* (Harcourt, Brace & World, 1967). His book, *Reading the Sphere: Essays on Contemporary Poetry* (Berkeley Hills Books, 2002) is a collection of essays that were originally published in *Poetry Flash.* His poetry collections include *Doubleness* (Heyday Books, 2000), *Totem Pole* (3300 Review Press, 1996), *The Fields* (Pennywhistle, 1990), and *Translucent Gears* (North Atlantic Books, 1982). His poetry has appeared in *The American Poetry Review, Denver Quarterly,* and other journals. His latest published book of poems is *Deconstruction of the Blues.*

Clare You

Clare You taught and coordinated the Korean language program as well as serving as Chair of the Center for Korean Studies. She is the recipient of the Korean Silver Medal of Culture in recognition of her contributions to Korean education abroad and cultural exchanges between Korea and the United States. Clare You has co-authored Korean textbooks, and she has been translating modern Korean poetry and fiction into English. Many of her translations of poems, short stories, essays, and research articles have appeared in magazines and journals in the U. S. and in Korea.

THE KOREAN VOICES SERIES

This Side of Time
Selected Poems by Ko Un
Translated by Claire You and Richard Silberg
Volume 16   978-1-935210-32-0   *100 pages* $16.00

Borderland Roads
Selected Poems of Ho Kyun
Translated by Ian Haight and T'ae-young Ho
Volume 15   978-1-935210-08-5   *102pages* $16.00

Scale and Stairs
Selected Poems of Heeduk Ra
Translated by Won-chung Kim and Christopher Merrill
Volume 14   978-1-893996-24-3   *88 pages* $17.00

One Human Family & Other Stories — Chung Yeun-hee
Translated by Hyun-jae Yee Sallee
Volume 13   978-1-893996-87-8   *232 pages* $16.00

Woman on the Terrace — Poems by Moon Chung-hee
Translated by Seong-kon Kim and Alec Gordon
Volume 12   978-1-87399686-1   *120 pages* $18.00

Eyes of Dew — Poems by Chonggi Mah
Translated by Brother Anthony of Taizé
Volume 11   1-893996-79-4$ *160 pages*   16.00

Even Birds Leave the World — Selected Poems of Ji-woo Hwang
Translated by Won-chun Kim & Christopher Merrill
Volume 10   1-893996-45-x   *104 pages* $14.00

The Depths of a Clam — Selected Poems of Kim Kwang-kyu
Translated by Brother Anthony of Taize
Volume 9   1-893996-43-3   *160 pages* $16.00